THE MODEL VILLAGE
AND ITS COTTAGES:
BOURNVILLE.

PLATE I. . . .
BLOCK OF FOUR
COTTAGES . . .
BOURNVILLE. . .

AND ITS COTTAGES:
BOURNVILLE

ILLUSTRATED BY
FIFTY-SEVEN PLATES OF PLANS, VIEWS, AND DETAILS

BY

W. ALEXANDER HARVEY
Architect.

LONDON
B. T. BATSFORD, 94, HIGH HOLBORN
NEW YORK: CHARLES SCRIBNER'S SONS
1906

DEDICATED TO

MR & MRS. GEORGE CADBURY.

PREFACE.

In February, 1904, I was invited to read a paper on the subject of Cottage Homes before the London Architectural Association, when I took as the basis of my remarks the work executed from my designs at the Bournville Village. In adapting myself to the limits of such a paper, I found that, while much which was treated suffered considerably through inevitable compression, a great deal that I wished also to include had to be omitted. This suggested to me the idea, now realised in book form, of treating the subject more comprehensively, giving plans and views of actual examples of cottages, with measurements and costs, and amplifying and adding to my former notes and observations.

Even with the larger scope of a book, it is still felt that much has been left undone and unsaid, and it is frankly admitted that one man dealing with his own work can scarcely pretend to do full justice to the broad subject under notice ; nevertheless, it is hoped that the plans and views of Bournville cottages, accompanied by descriptions and notes, may at least prove of value as suggestions for those interested in a matter now claiming very wide attention—that of the building of cottages which may fitly be called *homes*.

PREFACE.

I am indebted to the Bournville Village Trust for their courtesy in allowing me to publish plans and particulars of the Estate cottages, as well as to the private owners of the few other cottages dealt with in these pages. I must also acknowledge my indebtedness to Mr. T. B. Rogers for his valuable assistance in the production of the book.

W. ALEXANDER HARVEY.

5, BENNETT'S HILL,
      BIRMINGHAM
          December, 1905

CONTENTS.

CONTENTS

LIST OF PLATES.

LIST OF PLATES.

OTHER ILLUSTRATIONS

THE

MODEL VILLAGE: BOURNVILLE

INTRODUCTION.

In introducing the present work on "The Model Village and its Cottages," it would be certainly out of place to discuss the housing problem ; there is, nevertheless, an aspect of this question to which the attention of the reader should be briefly directed.

The housing problem is no longer one in which the poor in the congested districts of great towns are alone concerned. A far larger section of the people is affected,—a section which includes not only the labouring class, but also the skilled artisan, and even a class of the people still more prosperous. In the light of present sanitary and hygienic knowledge it is at last recognised that the housing conditions of the past will not suffice for the future. The difficulties besetting reform are necessarily very great, yet with the movement now afoot—not only in this country, but also on the Continent and in America—it is not unreasonable to expect that before long important changes will take place. Now that politicians and economists, as well as sanitarians, are identifying themselves with the movement, it is clear that if it is to result in lasting good, the attention of the *builders* of these new homes for the people must also be engaged , and the field that thus presents itself to the efforts of the architect is a large one.

B

No better testimony to this need can be afforded than by the typical latter-day artisan-suburb, and it is indeed in this very suburb that the housing problem confronts us in what threatens to be in the future one of its worst aspects   Desolate row upon row of ugly and cramped villas, ever multiplying to meet the demands of a quickly increasing population, where no open spaces are reserved, where trees and other natural beauties are sacrificed to the desire to crowd upon the land as many dwellings as possible, and where gardens cannot be said to exist—such are the suburbs which threaten to engulf our cities   That they do not adequately meet the needs of the people is beyond all question.

The remedy most frequently suggested is that the people should themselves undertake and develop housing schemes collectively through the municipalities.   It is pointed out that, if nothing is done, the municipalities will before long have a slum problem on the outskirts of the town to deal with, and it is urged that they should have greater power over the development of land in the extra-urban districts   It is recommended, again, that the authorities should exercise the powers they already possess.   The Inter-Departmental Committee on Physical Deterioration, in their Report to the Government of 1904, insisted most strongly, it will be remembered, on the necessity for preventing the creation of these new slums.   "The local authorities in contiguous areas which are in process of urbanisation," it declares, " should co-operate with a view to securing proper building regulations, in furtherance of which end the making of building bye-laws, to be approved by the Local Government Board, should be made compulsory on both urban and rural authorities ; attention should also be given to the preservation of open spaces, with abundance of light and air.   By the use of judicious foresight and prudence the growth of squalid slums may be arrested, and districts which hereafter become urbanised may have at least some of the attributes of an ideal garden city "

In the case of municipalities undertaking the development of land, emphasis should be laid upon the advisability of securing the services of experts both for the laying out of the land and for the designing of the houses, and in order to obtain variety in the latter it is recommended that the designs should be the work of several architects

At present, as is well known, the rows of houses in what has been called the artisan-suburb are usually the work of the speculating builder, who buys land at a cheap rate and builds to create ground rents, often selling the houses at a bare profit, or even under cost. As the maintenance of the property does not fall upon himself, it is not surprising that the class of building erected should be that generally known as " jerry-built "

Apart from these and other schemes suggested is the work of the Garden City Association in their experiment at Hitchin, and also the experiments at Port Sunlight, Bournville, and elsewhere, which have all given such a practical impetus to the movement. An encouraging sign of the times, too, is the commendable effort of the Trustees of Eton College, who, to prevent the development of the typical artisan-suburb on their extensive land at Hampstead, have formed a Trust to buy 240 acres for building purposes, the division of the land and the plans of the houses being required to meet certain specified conditions. In many suburbs, owing to the few houses of high rental, the rates are extremely high, and a heavy percentage is absorbed by the schools. One of the objects of the Garden Suburb, as it is called, is the amalgamation of all classes in the same district, the artisan and the well-to-do living in reasonable proximity to one another With the abolition of the unsightly row the æsthetic objection at least to such an arrangement is removed, for in the interesting disposition of houses of varying sizes lies one of the secrets of beautiful village building, as is testified in so many well-known old villages   In the new suburb it is hoped to provide cottages for workpeople with gardens of one tenth of an acre

But whether land is developed privately or by public bodies, it is essential, in order to secure real reform, that the needs, domestic and social, of the people for whom the houses are provided should be intimately understood.   What will have to be provided are *homes*, and it should be clearly recognised what constitutes the *home* demanded by the large section of the community which the problem affects.

At the outset it may be noted that for half the year the occupants of these homes spend the hours of recreation out of doors, also that most of them prefer that opportunities for such re-creation should be had within easy reach of the home itself.   Though the public-houses and the numerous artificial pleasures provided in towns are sought by so many, the persistence of those who still cultivate the contracted and ill-favoured garden strip suggests a need of the greatest importance.   This persistence, moreover, does not, it will be found, indicate a desire for exercise and fresh air alone, but a love for familiar surroundings   Among the lowest class this instinct may still be observed, and in court tenements it will be found that the doorstep takes the place of the garden strip. The fact is that the Englishman's house is his castle, and though his castle be deprived of its "grounds," the home instinct, so deeply rooted in the English character, will not be denied. Whether in the future this instinct should be fostered, or blunted as in the past, is a matter of elementary sociology.   The inference, then, will be that the accommodation of the house is not the only matter with which we have to concern ourselves, but that the closest attention should also be devoted to the environment. Besides the provision of an ample garden, the environment itself must be healthy and pleasant The influence of surroundings in exalting or depressing the mind, and thus affecting the life, is a matter not only for the theorist, but for the architect

With the provision of a garden, the tenant himself may add to the beauty of his home, and at the same time enjoy fresh air and recreation The cultivation of the soil is certainly the best antidote to the sedentary occupations of those working in large towns. A primitive instinct is indulged, the full value of which seems hardly yet to have been realised. Many believe, indeed, that with its encouragement the abuse of the social club and public-house will be materially lessened, and one of the greatest social evils of the time disappear. (The experience of Bournville certainly gives support to this conclusion, for nearly every householder there spends his leisure in gardening, and there is not a single licensed-house in the village)

With regard to the house itself, so far as it contributes to a pleasant environment, it should be remembered that architectural beauty is not dependent upon the ornament introduced , on the contrary, the use of the latter rather tends to deprive the dwelling of its homeliness, and of this truth the jerry-built house, with its scroll-cut lintel and moulded brick string-course, affords only too frequent an illustration. The soul of beauty is harmony, which may co-exist with the veriest simplicity ; and it is in the harmonious treatment of parts, and not in useless and sometimes costly decoration, that a dwelling gains that homely appearance which it should be our aim to realise.

The chief essentials in a home, then, are adequate accommodation —which must include a bath as a *sine quâ non*—a pleasing and harmonious appearance of exterior and environment, and the provision of an ample garden

It is surely not a mere coincidence that at the present time, not only in England but in other countries, a movement is in progress side by side with that of housing reform which is of great significance—the revival in domestic architecture. At present this has manifested itself chiefly in recent examples of country houses and in residences of the larger cottage class. Though the influence has already revealed itself to some extent even in the smaller cottage-dwellings, and though many notable experiments have been made—most telling of all the splendid experiment at Garden City—it may be said that the effort on the part of the architect generally to satisfy the demands both of art and economy has yet to be made. The fact that it is cheaper to erect villas in long rows of a repeated and stereotyped design has doubtless largely discouraged such effort, but the prejudice of the artisan and others against the revival—for the revival was at first looked upon, perhaps, as an artistic craze—can scarcely now be regarded as an obstacle If the needs of the people, as they have been conceived in the few preceding paragraphs, are to be satisfied, the two movements of housing reform and the revival in domestic architecture must certainly advance hand in hand With adequate experiment it will probably be found, moreover, that the difficulty on the economic side has been exaggerated On this account, in the examples of smaller cottage types here dealt with, attention has been specially paid to this aspect of the question, a pleasing appearance having been aimed at, with the employment of the least costly materials An effort has also been made in a further stage to show how monotony may be avoided, even with a repetition of the same plan, by variety in combination and disposition.

Larger types of cottages are also included, and economy in

design and cost of materials has here also been considered, as well as a pleasing effect aimed at The plans given, with one exception, are of examples actually existing, so that what defects may be present can scarcely be disguised. The intention is that they should be regarded chiefly as suggestive, and it is frankly admitted that they are not only capable of modification, by which their cost may be reduced, but also of improvement. The work dealt with has been executed during the last ten years.

The method of including with the description of each cottage such notes and suggestions as have seemed worthy of mention, has been adopted as being more valuable than grouping these under separate heads, though a number of general observations on various features of cottage-building has also been added.

The photographs reproduced were taken by T Lewis and by Harold Baker, both of Birmingham

NOTE.—-The cost is given of all cottages where the accommodation, materials, &c, are fully described, with the exception of one or two cases in which the cottages are owned privately As most of the examples given have been built by the Bournville Village Trust, it should be noted that the figures stated include an addition to the net cost of $3\frac{1}{4}$ per cent. as builder's profit.

PLATE II.
THE TRIANGLE,
BOURNVILLE.

THE BOURNVILLE VILLAGE.

ALTHOUGH many articles have already appeared from time to time in newspaper and periodical respecting the Bournville Village, the following account of its founding and development will doubt-less be of interest to the reader —

In 1879 Messrs Cadbury Brothers removed their works from Birmingham to the present site at Bournville, and twenty-four cottages were erected there for their workmen This really formed the nucleus out of which in recent years the village has developed. It was in 1895 that Mr. George Cadbury, the senior member of the present firm, commenced the work of building a model village One of the objects of the scheme was that of " alleviating the evils which arise from the insanitary and insufficient housing accommo-dation supplied to large numbers of the working classes, and of securing to workers in factories some of the advantages of outdoor village life, with opportunities for the natural and healthful occupation of cultivating the soil." A simple and interesting statement of the motive behind the experiment was made by Mr. Cadbury himself at the Garden City Conference, held at Bournville in 1901. An intimate knowledge of the lives of Birmingham working-men, gained by an experience of some forty years, had shown him that the greatest drawback to their moral and physical progress was the lack of any healthful occupation for their leisure. Although many men took up carpentry and other crafts, such hobbies, he said, had proved insufficiently recreative, and in most cases the men soon tired of them. Realising this, he began to think of new means. His conclusion was that the only practical thing was to bring the factory worker out on to the land, that he might pursue the most natural and healthful of all recreations, that of gardening It was impossible for working men to be healthy and have healthy children, when after being confined all day in factories they spent their evenings in an institute, club room, or public house. If it were necessary for their health, as it undoubtedly was, that they should get fresh air, it was equally to the advantage of their moral life that they should be brought into contact with Nature. There was an advantage, too, in bringing the working-man on to the land, for, instead of his losing money in the amusements usually sought in the towns, he saved it in his garden produce—a great consideration where the poorer class of workman was concerned The average yield per garden in the 1901 tests at Bournville, after making allowance for all outgoings, proved to be 1s 11d each per week Mr Cadbury also thought that the increased consumption of fresh vegetable food, instead of animal food, was further desirable It was touching, he thought, to see the interest and pleasure taken by town families when on coming into the country they saw seeds germinate and vegetables grown for the first time. Nor was the advantage of leaving the town for the country restricted to the workmen Mr. Cadbury showed that the greater facilities there for obtaining land were also of advantage to the manufacturer whose business was increasing.

The Bournville idea was at first regarded as an impracticable one, even apart from the economic side of the question, but the realisation of the scheme has proved otherwise The average garden space allotted to the Bournville cottages is 600 square yards, this being as much as most men can conveniently cultivate,

PLATE IV.

LINDEN ROAD,
BOURNVILLE.

PLATE V.

and, almost without exception, the Bournville tenants are the
most enthusiastic gardeners — a statement no one surely will
traverse who has paid a visit to the village in the summer.

While it was the first aim of the founder to provide dwellings
for the factory worker which should have adequate accommodation
and large gardens, it was not intended that at Bournville provision
should be made alone for the poorer working class. It might be
pointed out that one of the most prominent ideals in the scheme
of the Garden Suburb Trust, already referred to, is "that all classes
may live in kindly neighbourliness," and the amalgamation of the
factory-worker and the brain-worker in the same district is catered
for as being expressly desirable At Bournville there has always
been a demand for houses both on the part of the skilled artisan
and others, and this demand has been provided for from the
first. Rents in the village range from 4s 6d. a week, rates not
included, to 12s a week , and there are also a few houses of a still
larger class at higher rentals Nor are the houses let to Messrs.
Cadbury's own workpeople exclusively, as the following figures will
show—figures based on a private census taken during 1901, and
here quoted from a booklet issued by the Village Trust ·—

Proportion of Householders working in—		Occupations of Householders—	
Bournville	41 2 per cent.	Employed at indoor work in factories	50 7 per cent
Villages within a mile of Bournville	18 6 ,,	Clerks and travellers	13 3 ,,
Birmingham	40 2 ,,	Mechanics, carpenters, bricklayers, and various occupations not admitting of exact classification	36 0 ,,

The village is four miles from Birmingham, and is easily
accessible by cycle, rail, or electric car. The last come within easy
distance of the village, workmen s fares being 2d. return.

Under the founder's first scheme the land was let upon leases of 999 years, subject to a ground rent varying from $\frac{1}{2}$d. to 1d per yard (600 square yards at $\frac{1}{2}$d. and 1d. = £1 5s. and £2 10s. respectively) Arrangements were made to find capital on mortgages granted at the rate of Three per cent to those who paid less than half the cost of the house and Two and a-half per cent to those who paid more Although a stipulation was made that no one person should be allowed to build more than four houses, it was found necessary to revise the arrangement in order to prevent speculation. In 1900, therefore, the estate was handed over to a Trust on behalf of the nation, the whole income to be directed to solving the housing problem. The houses now built are let to tenants at moderate weekly rentals, which include the annual ground rent, equal to about 1d per yard (according to its value), and which should yield Four per cent. net The revenue of house and ground rents is employed, after provision has been made for the maintenance and repair of present property, in the development of the village itself, and in the laying out and development of other villages elsewhere, the Trust being empowered under the deed of foundation to acquire land in any part of Great Britain Subsequently to the formation of the Trust, additional land adjacent to Bournville has been added to the founder's gift, and included in the village, which now extends over 458 acres Already upwards of 100 acres of land have been laid out for building. There are now about 450 houses in the hands of the Trust, which number, added to the 143 sold under the first scheme, makes a total of nearly 600 With the income of the Trust, building is being steadily proceeded with, and there is a continual demand for houses.

The Trustees have power to make arrangements with railways and other companies for cheap means of transit. They may lease,

PLATE VI.
SYCAMORE ROAD,
BOURNVILLE.

PLATE VII.
THE SCHOOLS,
BOURNVILLE.
SEE PAGE 13.

PLATE VIII. . .
CARVED STONE
PANELS FOR
SCHOOLS. . .

underlet, or sell land, or develop it and prepare it for building, give land, or erect buildings for places of worship, hospitals, schools, technical institutes, libraries, gymnasiums, laundries, baths, &c. Occupying a central position in the village are already the Bournville Meeting House (see plates X. and XI), the Ruskin Hall, an institute founded in 1903, and including library, reading-room, lecture hall, class rooms (see plate IX), and the schools described later. Ample open spaces have been reserved in various parts of the village. These include the Village Green ; The Triangle (a plot of land with lawn, flower beds, and shrubbery, intersected by public paths — see plate II.), Camp Wood (an undulating woodland, thick with old forest-trees) ; children's playgrounds and lawns, with swings, bars, &c. , allotment gardens ; youths' and girls' gardens (consisting of a number of small plots rented and cultivated by boys and girls, in connection with which gardening classes are held), &c A large area of land, through which flows the Bourn stream, has also been reserved for laying out as a public park. Adjacent to the Estate, though not part of it, are two extensive and well-wooded recreation grounds belonging to Messrs Cadbury, which are put at the disposal of their men and women employees , those for the former including open-air swimming baths, which may be used during stipulated hours by the tenants of the Estate houses These recreation grounds separate the works buildings from the village itself, and in the event of the factory ceasing to exist, the Trust deed provides that they be handed over to the District Council for use as a public park. Nearly all the old trees and woodland on the Estate have been preserved, and new trees planted in many parts.

The schools (see plate VII.) are the gift to the village of Mr and Mrs George Cadbury They accommodate 540 children

(270 boys and 270 girls), and are constructed on the central-hall plan There are six class-rooms for fifty children each, and six for forty each, and the dimensions of the large hall are 84 ft. by 32 ft. The land falls from North to South, and advantage has been taken of the basement afforded to provide for accommodation for classes in cookery, laundry, manual instruction, and various branches of handicraft The buildings stand in grounds two and a-half acres in extent, adjoining which is the Park, the children thus having access in all to about ten acres. The tower rises to a height of about 60 ft , and has been utilised for a library, laboratory, &c. An extensive view of the surrounding country is obtained from the top, and a map, incised in stone, with compass and locating apparatus, is provided for instructing the children in local geography. Everything is being done in the designing of details —carved and painted panels, &c.—to make the building itself a permanent means of educating the children ; the subjects chosen include historical scenes, truthfully depicted as regards dress, customs, architecture, &c , while in the bosses and voussoirs are represented English flowers and foliage, conventionally treated. The carving is executed by Mr Benjamin Creswick, of Birmingham

In the designing of the building every effort has been made to embody the latest improvements and the result of the most broad-minded and enlightened study of education.

Gardens are provided for the instruction of the children in gardening, vegetable growing, &c.

The low death-rate at Bournville during 1904 of 6·9 per thousand, compared with 19 per thousand in Birmingham, is some indication of the healthiness of the village The figures are taken from the report of the district medical officer of health

It is not proposed to deal here with the economics of model-village or garden-city schemes generally. Though the movement

PLATE IX.
RUSKIN HALL,
BOURNVILLE.

PLATE X. . . .
MEETING HOUSE,
BOURNVILLE. . .

is still very young, it is already advancing from the problematical stage. Its progress is being watched with the keenest interest by many who realise that of all courses the most impracticable in the long run is that which allows the slum-suburb to spring up unchecked.

If it be asked, with regard to the problem of the housing of the people, what is Bournville's contribution towards its solution, it would be stating its claims at the lowest to say that it stands as an example of what the village of the future may be, a village of healthy homes amid pleasant surroundings, where fresh air is abundant and beauty present, and where are secured to its people by an administration co-operative in nature numerous benefits which under present conditions are denied them elsewhere.

COTTAGES AT £135, with Notes on the Economic Building of Small Cottages.

PLATES XII AND XIII

COTTAGES IN BLOCKS OF EIGHT, AT £135

PLATE XII gives the plan, with elevation, of a block of eight cottages, the accommodation of which is the least, and the dimensions the lowest, that should be provided for homes with one living room

The accommodation is as follows —

GROUND FLOOR

Living Room, 12 ft 4 in. × 13 ft   Kitchen, 8 ft × 12 ft 6 ins (with "Cabinet" Bath, and boiler with patent steam exhaust)   Larder under stairs

BEDROOM FLOOR

First Bedroom, 9 ft 2 ins × 13 ft, and recess   Second Bedroom, 8 ft 4 ins × 11 ft 2 ins   Third Bedroom, 7 ft 6 ins × 8 ft

Total cost, £135 per cottage

Laying out of garden, £7 10s extra

Cubical contents, 64,800 ft at 4d. per foot cube = £1,080 per block, or £135 per cottage.

There has been considerable discussion of late with regard to the building of cheap cottages suitable for labourers and the poorer artisans, both in the country and elsewhere   Experiments have been made in which the building materials employed have been other than brick, the object being a reduction in cost   The bye-laws which do not at present sanction the erection of cottages in some of these materials will, it is hoped, before long be altered. Meanwhile, what is wanted in most districts is the cheap dwelling in brick.

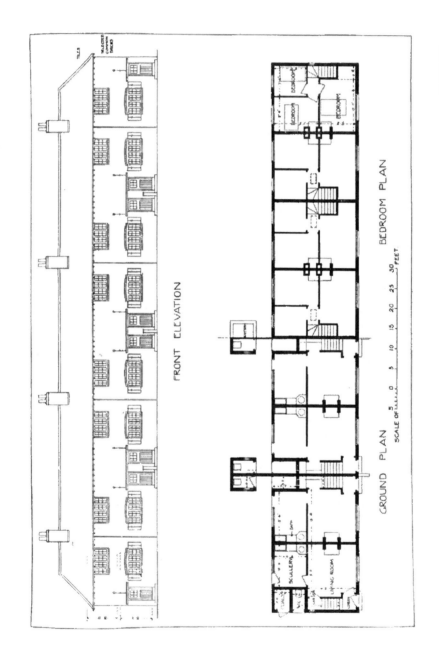

FRONT ELEVATION

BEDROOM PLAN

GROUND PLAN

SCALE OF FEET

PLATE XII.
COTTAGES IN

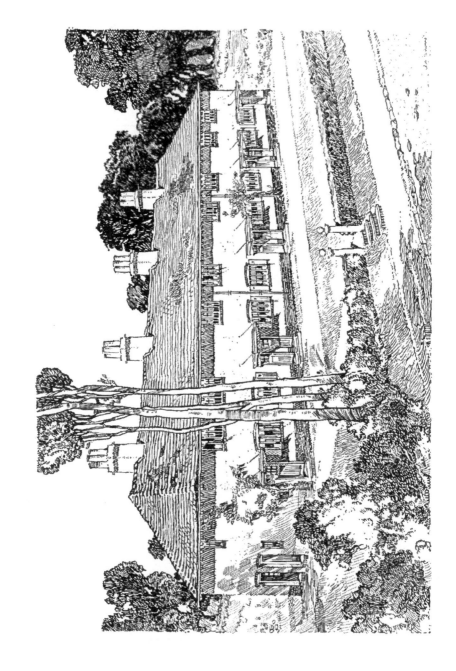

The example here given is of a similar plan to one from which a number of cottages in blocks of *four* have been erected at Bournville. Owing to a decision on the part of the Village Trust not to build in blocks of more than four, the plans here given have never been carried out at Bournville, but in view of the danger there is of under-estimating the cost of such cottages, and the importance of avoiding inaccuracies, estimates have been obtained for their erection under similar conditions. Economy of construction has been the main object in the design, without sacrificing that pleasant environment, privacy and homeliness of appearance which are, as already indicated, essential to the cottage home

The cost of erecting in blocks of four only is necessarily increased, and the lowest estimate for those at Bournville is £160 per cottage, the particular estimate being, however, for a block of four on "made up" ground, necessitating deep footings, the cottages including the sunk bath, which is more costly than the "Cabinet" patent.

The plan might be simplified, if desired, by omitting the division wall between the living room and scullery, thus making one large room. The boiler, sink, and bath might then be planned in a small recess which could be screened off by a curtain when not in use.

SIMPLICITY AND REGULARITY OF PLANNING —The roof runs uninterruptedly from end to end, by which unnecessary roof complications are avoided, the chimneys have been grouped together to diminish trimming and flashing, always costly items, and have been brought to the highest point in the roof to prevent smoky flues, consequent upon down draughts, and the building throughout is of a very inexpensive character. Further, the eaves run uninterruptedly, for the windows are not allowed to complicate

the spouting and roofing by breaking through the roof, the
wall-plate nevertheless being kept at a fairly low level In all
cottages of this class, compactness and regularity should be
always aimed at in planning, and the wall lines—set out at right
angles—should be as long and unbroken as possible.

ARRANGEMENT OF OUTBUILDINGS.—The w.c.'s, here isolated,
are in the Bournville blocks of four planned under the main roof,
which arrangement is for many reasons preferable As many as
possible of the outbuildings should, in the case of small cottages,
be arranged under the main roof. Often, where the outbuildings
of these rows of cottages are extensive, one or more of the houses
suffers through the projecting eaves of the other, and there is
a narrow outlook upon a cramped yard. The better view of the
garden obtained from the back rooms by the avoidance of this is
an important consideration. The kitchen, in small property, is as
much used as the living room, and the value of the restful glimpse
of green to the housewife should not be ignored (The isolation
of the w.c. in the example under notice does not obstruct the
light.) In the case of a corner site it is preferable to close in
the yard at the back of the house, so that the week's wash may
not be exposed to the public view. It may be advanced, however,
that such a domestic display is not really unsightly, but gives a
pleasant human interest to the surroundings Such an opinion,
nevertheless, will probably not find general acceptance.

HEIGHTS OF ROOMS.—The height of the building will also be
reduced to the lowest limit The heights of 8 ft. 3 ins for the
ground floor, and 8 ft for the chamber floor, are quite adequate
for the average cottage. so long as sufficient ventilation is provided.
There is some difficulty in getting the artisan to recognise this,
for a lofty and often draughty and cold room seems to have an
unaccountable attraction for him. As, however, floor space is the

essential, the reduction of heights is in every way a legitimate means of economising the brickwork ; moreover, the scale of the building is at the same time rendered more pleasing With the height reduced, it will be necessary to introduce the casement window, as the sash kind requires a loftier elevation. This, however, will be no detriment, as the former is more agreeable and appropriate to the cottage home.

EXTRA BEDROOM ACCOMMODATION.—If in any of the smaller types of cottages dealt with it is thought desirable to provide a fourth bedroom, or if larger bedrooms are required, an attic might be provided by slightly lifting the roof (where this is necessary), and the first floor might then be divided into two rooms or not, according to the requirements. Staircases, however, are expensive, and it is well for the sake of economy to provide bedrooms on the first floor. Where roof space is available this may be used for lumber, when the trap by which it is reached should be placed in the least important bedroom. The ceiling, however, should be slightly strengthened, and the bearing should not be too great

ORNAMENT —The sound principle that beauty should be based on utility is often violated, even in the building of small cottages and villas, in order to gratify a vulgar taste for shoddy and meaningless display Although the architect may not be entirely to blame for submitting to this preference, it is none the less certain that if he avail himself of such opportunities as occur to introduce a purer taste, the public will in time respond, while such efforts on his part will be always heartily approved by his fellow architects. The difficulty of inducing builders to stock ornament that is really good is merely one of demand. The public taste may after all be found to be more amenable than is commonly represented. A readiness on the part of the Bournville tenants to catch the spirit of homely simplicity suggested in the design of the houses has shown itself in the manner in which they furnish their homes, as, for instance, in their use of suitable curtains for the casement windows

If it be decided that a row of cottages should have ornament, this should not be too small or crowded, and should be introduced in the right place — in the case of eight cottages, say in the third and the sixth, the unadorned ones serving as a foil   An excess of ornament should be avoided, especially if the aim is economy, and what there is should be broad and simple, for such, happily, is increasingly in favour in preference to the incongruous and florid stock carving of the jerry builder, which, bad as it is, must yet cost something   If money is to be spent, let preference be given first of all to the quality of the material used, and then to the extra elaboration of such material, such as roughcast, parquetry, colour decoration, etc.

While the appearance of the elevation of the blocks of eight cottages here given is improved by the introduction over the doors of hoods with wrought-iron stays, the erection of two large posts with a horizontal cross-piece as a support for honeysuckle or climbing rose is not only cheaper, but is in the circumstances a more suitable way of adorning what is of necessity a plain elevation. The steps before the doorway should then be cut short without returns, to enable the plant to be set as near as possible to the posts   The two steps are a necessity in order to secure good ventilation beneath the floors, where boarded floors are used.

THE TRUE TEST OF ECONOMY —Many jerrybuilt houses are the work of the speculating builder, who immediately on their completion sells them to one who buys to sell again.   He secures himself, but with such inferior property someone must in the end suffer considerable loss.   To say that a house has been built on economic lines because the cost of erection has been the lowest

possible is to mislead, for the true test of economy is that which
will take into account the cost of repairs at the end of ten years,
and its then value. In designing cottages for an estate or garden
city, the architect will therefore realise the importance of building
dwellings that shall be lasting He will perceive that to take the
low cost of the jerrybuilt house as a standard will only lead him
ultimately into endless trouble and expense He will not, to save
a trifling initial cost, incur a heavier one later on, for in this case
the ownership of the house does not change, and maintenance is
not a thing that can be shirked.

FOUNDATIONS —He will therefore see that there is a bed of
concrete over the whole site, that his floors are well ventilated by
allowing a good space between the under-side of ground floor
joists and ground work, that the damp course is effectual, and
also that plenty of air-bricks are inserted to ensure through
ventilation, thus providing against the growth of dry-rot and all
the expense it entails.

As the tenants of the cottages will doubtless be amateur
gardeners who will probably add manure to the soil each year, the
damp course is likely to get covered over ; it is therefore essential
that this should be at least six inches above the ground when the
cottages are built

STOCK ARTICLES —Economy may always be exercised by using
what are *worthy* stock-articles of building, and in the case of a
model village, where large orders will be given, the architect
should make it his business to introduce new lines—moulds,
doors, grates, mantels, etc —the quality of which is first well
proved Stock sizes of building materials should be selected,
and the planning should be adapted to them to avoid waste. For
instance, joists should always be of such sizes as will prevent waste
in the cutting of timbers. Joists are stocked in a definite number

of foot lengths.   Rooms of 12 ft. 4 ins. width, with 4 ins bearing allowed at each end, will require joists of 13 ft lengths, in which case there is no waste ; on the other hand, rooms with 12 ft. 6 ins. width, with the same bearing, will require 14 ft. joist lengths, in which case 10 ins. in timber and the labour in cutting will be wasted, which the extra 2 ins gained does not warrant; 12 ft. 4 ins., 13 ft. 4 ins., 14 ft. 4 ins., and so on, are therefore preferable dimensions.   Again, if the size of the joists be 9 ins × 3 ins, 27 ins. cube is obtained, which is not stronger than 11 ins × 2 ins., giving 22 ins. cube.   If the latter be chosen, therefore, 5 ins cube are saved   True, the house will be raised in height, but not sufficiently to appreciably increase the cost   This is only one instance of how selection of material may be profitably studied

GENERAL.—In the example given the staircase runs between the houses, and gives them a good wide frontage, bringing the outer houses nearer to the extremity of the land, and enabling a more convenient division of the gardens.   It will be noticed that the bath in these small cottages is the "Cabinet" patent, which is strongly recommended on account of its being easily shut up and stowed away (see page 51).   The interior fittings are of the simplest and most inexpensive kind, such a thing as the ingle-nook, however pleasing and comfortable, being reserved for a better class of cottage.   Ample cupboard room, nevertheless, is provided, and it should be noted that such conveniences as cloak rails, cup-rails and hooks, picture rails, etc., are fixed in all the cottages dealt with.   Small gas cookers or grills should be included in all cottages, whether large or small.   White's patent steam exhaust should also be fitted in all cottages

THE LAYING OUT OF GARDENS.

The garden, a feature of such importance in the model village,

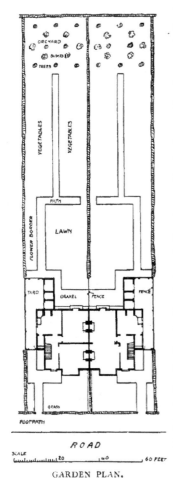

GARDEN PLAN.

or garden city, should have no less care and attention in the planning than the house itself. The accompanying plan is one frequently adopted at Bournville where the aspect is suitable. The arrangement is modified in the case of the smallest cottages by the reduction or omission of turf. The bedding, with the various trees and shrubs supplied, is indicated on the plan.

With the large garden-space allotted, the paths should be broad and, generally speaking, planned in straight lines, the width being not less than 3 ft.—even 4 ft. not being too wide. At Bournville they are made of 6 ins. of ashes and 3 ins. of gravel. Where there is turf the path should run at one extremity of the garden plot, giving the full width remaining for as spacious a lawn as possible. At the bottom of the lawn it might be turned to the left or right, as the case may be, as far as the centre, and carried down through the kitchen garden so that the fruit trees and vegetables may be easily accessible on either hand. With a south aspect, however, it is

advisable to still continue the path down one side, the shadow
of the adjacent hedge thus being cast not on the beds but on
the path itself. It should be borne in mind that in laying out
the beds all peas and beans, raspberry canes, etc , are best planted
north and south in order that the whole length of the rows may
get the sun. The tendency is for amateur gardeners to favour
winding paths, by which space is lost, besides the arrangement
being inconvenient. The curved line is rarely in harmony with
the setting of the cottage, and curves, if introduced, should be
gained rather in the planting of trees or flowers, curves in colour
being more pleasing

The number of trees, etc , provided in each of the Bournville
gardens is :—eight apple and pear trees, assorted according to the
nature of the soil, which, in addition to bearing fruit, form a
desirable screen between houses which are back to back ; twelve
gooseberry bushes, one Victoria plum, six creepers for the house,
including Gloire de Dijon and William Allen Richardson roses,
wistaria, honeysuckle, clematis, ivy in a number of varieties,
Ampelopsis veitchii, white and yellow jasmine, etc., according to the
aspect, as well as one or two forest trees, so placed as to frame the
building Hedges of thorn divide the houses, and form road
boundaries. The choice of trees and creepers is determined not
only by the suitability of soil or aspect, but also by the general
effect gained

E

FRONT ELEVATION

SCALE OF [10 5 10 15 20 25 30] FEET

GROUND PLAN   BEDROOM PLAN

PLATE XIV. . .
BLOCK OF FOUR
COTTAGES. SEE
PAGE 25. . . .

BLOCKS, PAIRS, AND SINGLE COTTAGES.

PLATES XIV AND XV
BLOCK OF FOUR COTTAGES

In the ascending scale we now come to a block of four, containing houses of two classes. The cost of each is approximately the same, and the advantages are about equal The outside houses have a side entrance with lobby and outer porch, thereby making the front room quite private, while in the inside ones the front door opens into the room, which has, however, the advantage of being more spacious.

Use of the Ingle Nook in Small Cottages.—The intro duction of an ingle nook in this latter secures to it a greater degree of comfort, and privacy from the road is also gained by the extension of the screen. Complete privacy may be secured by attaching a rod from the screen to the outside wall and dropping a curtain. The ingle is lighted by borrowed light from the half-glass door, the light passing through the glazed wooden screen In this case the ingle nook may be said to be the natural outcome of the plan The staircase in these inside houses is at the side of the ingle, and affords space beneath for a cupboard, which is reached from the kitchen. The staircase in the outside houses is approached near the window of the living room, and admits of space in like manner for a larder, which is entered from the lobby.

Ventilation.—It will be seen that the larder, in the case of the two middle houses, is arranged *within* the house, between the coals and the living room. Larders, wherever possible, should have an outside window, but in this case ventilation is very easily obtained in the following manner ·—An inlet of a 9-in. pipe enters the larder on the floor level from air bricks in the front wall, while in the coals at the back a concrete division is inserted at a height of 5 ft 6 ins or 5 ft. 9 ins. (the ground floor of the house from floor

E 2

to ceiling being in this instance 8 ft. 6 ins) Through a fanlight above the outside door of coals not only is light obtained, but, by means of a cord and pulley worked from the larder, through venti- lation also, while there is no danger of the invasion of coal dust

In both houses there is little space wasted In the outside ones the living rooms are entered immediately from the lobby, and the bedrooms immediately from a small landing, while there is a useful closet over the stairs, entered from the front bedroom.

The projection in this block gives variety to the street, and is the natural outcome of the requirements of the houses. The type is self-contained, and privacy is secured to the householders by the introduction of the side entrance to the outside houses, and by the arrangement of the doorways to the middle ones at the remote ends.

MATERIALS.—Brindled bricks, hand-made tiles, and casement windows of wood are here used, and the brickwork of the kitchen is pointed for whitewashing, with a 4-ft dado of paint. In these smaller cottages it is advisable to employ papers for interior wall decoration in preference to colour-wash, the latter being very soon soiled where there are children. Picture rails should be used in all cottages, if only to save the plaster.

ACCOMMODATION —The accommodation of the respective houses is as follows :—

GROUND FLOOR

	OUTSIDE HOUSES	INSIDE HOUSES
Living Room	12 ft 4 ins × 13 ft	15 ft × 16 ft 4 ins
Kitchen	10 ft 6 ins × 11 ft	11 ft × 11 ft. 3 ins
Tools, w c , and Coals		

BEDROOM FLOOR.

First Bedroom	12 ft 4 ins × 13 ft	13 ft 3 ins × 15 ft
Second Bedroom	8 ft × 11ft	6 ft 3 ins × 14 ft 2 ins.
Third Bedroom	7 ft 6 ins × 7 ft 10 ins	7 ft 9 ins × 8 ft 4 ins
Linen Closet		

PLATE XV.
BLOCK OF FOUR
COTTAGES. SEE
PAGE 26.

Total cost, including all extras and builder's profit, £872 per block, or £218 per cottage. Laying out of gardens, £10 per cottage.

Cubical contents, 48,295 ft. at 4⅓d. per foot cube, £872, or £218 per cottage.*

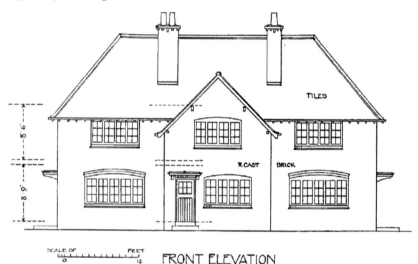

FRONT ELEVATION

BLOCK OF THREE COTTAGES.

The elevation shown in the accompanying illustration is of a block of three cottages, the two outside ones of which are similar to those shown on the foregoing plan. This is an example of how the same plan may be repeated with varied effect, or where there is not sufficient land for four.

* *NOTE.*—As most of the examples given have been built by the Bournville Village Trust, it should be noted that the figures stated include in all cases an addition to the net cost of 3¾% as builder's profit.

Where there is any marked difference in the price per foot cube not accounted for by more complicated planning, or by the better quality of materials, this is due, not only to the fluctuation of building prices during the last few years, but also to the variation in the cost of building at different periods of the year.

The extras include fencing, garden gates, etc.

PLATES XVI AND XVII
PAIR OF COTTAGES

VARIATION OF FORMER PLAN.—The plan shown in Plate xvi.
and illustrated in Plate xvii., is of a pair similar to the *outside*
cottages of Plate xiv. This again shows how it is possible to
play on the same plan in the building of a village, and so gain the
desirable variety of elevation The roof is hipped and covered
with pantiles A bay window is introduced in both the storeys,
with rough-cast between A rainwater cistern to store all roof
water is placed over the coals, which projects from the main block
A greater privacy is obtained by this slight projection, without
interfering with the light at the back. The chimneys are grouped
together in the centre, there being only one stack to both the
houses, which is carried to the highest point of the roof

Total cost of cottages built to this plan, including all extras,
£230 per cottage

Laying out of gardens, £10 per cottage

Cubical contents, 22,000 ft at 5*d* per foot cube, £460, or
£230 per cottage.

PLATE XVIII
PAIR OF COTTAGES

The plan and elevation shown on this plate are of an alternative
arrangement to the last. The houses have an entrance at the front
and an extended larder, owing to the staircases ascending from the
lobby The fireplaces are arranged in the corners of the rooms

PLATE XIX

The view here given shows three pairs of cottages built to the
plan shown on Plate xvi., and illustrates how a variety of
elevation may be gained by adding bays, dormers, etc, and by
using differing materials.

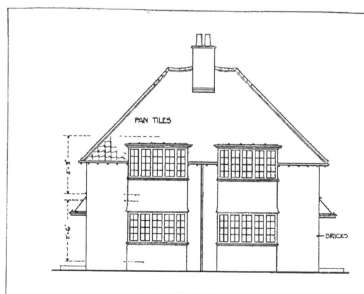

PAN TILES

BRICKS

FRONT ELEVATION

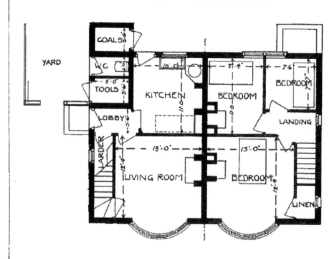

YARD

COALS

W.C.

TOOLS

KITCHEN

BEDROOM

BEDROOM

LOBBY

LANDING

LARDER

LIVING ROOM

BEDROOM

LINEN

GROUND PLAN   BEDROOM PLAN

SCALE OF   FEET

0   12

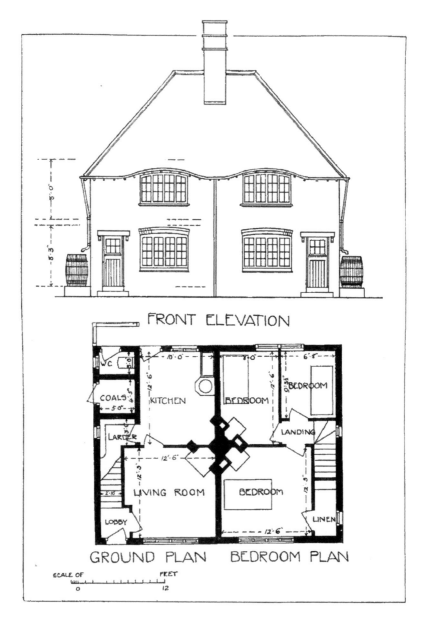

FRONT ELEVATION

GROUND PLAN   BEDROOM PLAN

SCALE OF   FEET

0   12

PLATE XVIII

PLATE XIX.
SEE PAGE 28.

DESCRIPTION OF PLATE XX

F

30

PLATE XX
PAIR OF COTTAGES

VARIATION OF FORMER PLAN.—This plate shows the development and variation of the *inside* houses of the block of four shown on Plate xiv., with a superior arrangement of larder, and with projecting coals The long sloping roof has been hipped back to give a pleasing line, especially in perspective

THE LONG SLOPING ROOF —The long sloping roof, a feature frequently introduced at Bournville, has several advantages. If it were not employed, and the front walls were carried up level with the ceiling line of the bedroom, the proportions of the elevation would not be so happy, while an additional expense would be incurred by the extra brickwork Such a height, moreover, would be wholly unnecessary In the case of cottages with the long sloping roof the height of bedrooms to the point of intersection of roof and wall need only be 5 ft. 6 ins. Ample ventilation is obtained by the simple insertion of a 9 in by 7 in air-brick on the outside wall, and a Sheringham ventilator or tobin tube within, about 5 ft 6 ins from the floor, the cost of the latter being about 3s, and of the former a little more. The long sloping roof can rarely be treated tastefully without boldly projecting the eaves. The projection gives a verandah in front of the house which affords a pleasant shelter. Wooden posts may be used as supports, and by training climbing plants up them, and allowing them to festoon, a really delightful summer bower may be formed As the roof is broad, pantiles may be used with safety so far as good taste is concerned : bold roof, bold covering By omitting the gutters at the dormer eaves a pleasing effect is gained, and gutters are quite unnecessary with an eaves projection. The cheeks of the dormers should be dressed with lead The cottages in question are whitewashed, and

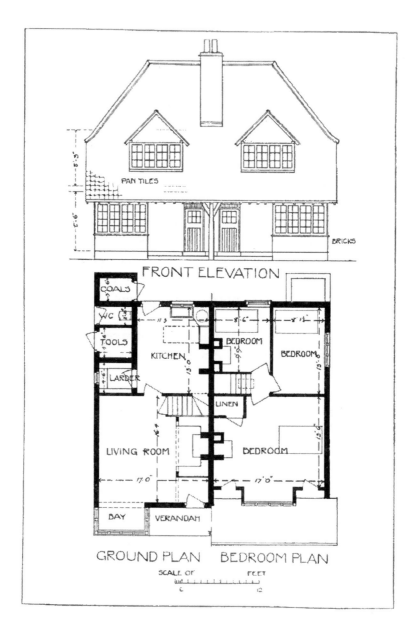

FRONT ELEVATION

PAN TILES

BRICKS

COALS

W.C.

TOOLS

KITCHEN

LARDER

LIVING ROOM

BAY

VERANDAM

BEDROOM

BEDROOM

LINEN

BEDROOM

GROUND PLAN   BEDROOM PLAN

SCALE OF   FEET

PLATE XX

have a tarred plinth of about 2 ft. to prevent the unsightliness of mud splashes

THE LARGE LIVING ROOM —In view of the gain to health of one spacious living-room over the parlour plan, a number of these cottages has been built in varying design at Bournville, and no difficulty has been found in letting them. There has been, however, considerable discussion with regard to their convenience to the artisan in other districts where they have been introduced Although cottages in the past had no third room, there having been, as here, one large comfortable room (often with the ingle nook) and a small kitchen at the back—all the accommodation really required—yet at the present time many artisans are not content without the useless parlour, which they appear to think adds dignity to the house, but which is used by them chiefly as a store-room for gim-cracks. There is, perhaps, a reasonable objection to a single large living-room on the part of a particular class who let the front room to a lodger. Nevertheless, for a model village or a garden city it is strongly recommended that the plan should be adopted freely, and the preference for the useless front-room in small cottages discouraged.

Total cost of the example given, including all extras, £268 per cottage

Laying out of gardens, £10 each.

Cubical contents, 28,587 ft, at $4\frac{1}{2}$d per foot cube, £536, or £268 per cottage.

Instances of the last two types of cottages dealt with appear in the view given on Plate IV

PLATE XXI
PAIR OF COTTAGES

THE smaller cottage shown here is planned on similar lines to
the foregoing, but with the additional accommodation of an attic,
and bay windows to the two storeys. This is an instance of how
a smaller cottage may be joined to a larger one in treating a corner
site, the larger one on the corner giving importance to each road.

PLATES XXII, XXIII, I (FRONTISPIECE), XXIV, XXV, AND XXVI
BLOCKS OF FOUR

THESE plates show examples of cottages in blocks of four rather
larger in size than the last type, and treated in different materials
Plate xxvi. shows the details of the cottages on Plate xxv.

PLATE XXIII.
BLOCK OF FOUR
COTTAGES. SEE
PAGE 32.

PLATE XXIV.
BLOCK OF FOUR
COTTAGES. SEE
PAGE 32.

PLATE XXVI.
DETAIL VIEW.
SEE PAGE 32

G

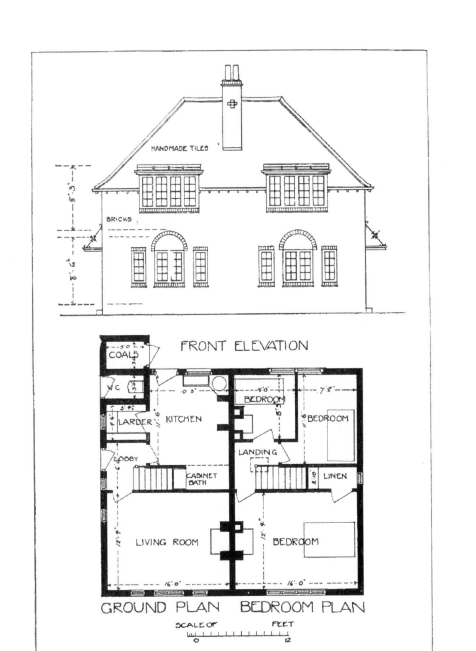

HANDMADE TILES

BRICKS

8'-3"

6'-6"

FRONT ELEVATION

COALS

W.C

LARDER   KITCHEN

BEDROOM

BEDROOM

LOBBY

LANDING

CABINET
BATH

LINEN

LIVING ROOM

BEDROOM

16'0"

16'0"

GROUND PLAN   BEDROOM PLAN

SCALE OF   FEET
0   12

PLATE XXVII

PAIR OF COTTAGES

PLATE XXVII gives the plan and elevation of a pair of cottages also having similar accommodation to those with the long sloping roofs shown on Plate xx. The cost, however, is here considerably reduced by each house having a side entrance, and by the omission of the ingle nook, verandah and bay, while the living room, though smaller, is not a passage room By approaching the stairs from the lobby, not only is more privacy secured, but the space beneath is made available in the kitchen for a " Cabinet " bath, which is so placed as to occupy it when in use instead of projecting into the kitchen. The planning is simple and square, which, with the omission of bays and the introduction of plain casements, all helps to reduce the cost

The accommodation is :—

GROUND FLOOR.

Living Room, 12 ft 4 ins × 16 ft Kitchen, 10 ft 3 ins × 11 ft 6 ins. Lobby Larder, w c and Coals

BEDROOM FLOOR.

First Bedroom, 12 ft 4 ins × 16 ft Second Bedroom, 7 ft 8 ins. × 11 ft 6 ins Third Bedroom, 8 ft × 8 ft 3 ins Linen Closet

Total cost, including all extras, £250 per cottage

Laying out of gardens, £10 each.

Cubical contents, 24,000 ft , at 5d. per foot cube, £500, or £250 per cottage.

PLATE XXVIII
PAIR OF COTTAGES

THIS plate shows the plan and elevation of a pair of cottages having the parlour in addition to the living room and scullery The living room, which should always be the larger, is here the full width of the house. The measurements are :—

GROUND FLOOR.

> Living Room, 11 ft 5 ins × 16 ft 6 ins   Parlour, 11 ft 4 ins × 13 ft 3 ins Scullery, Outside Larder, w c and Coals

BEDROOM FLOOR

> First Bedroom, 11 ft 4 ins × 13 ft 5 ins   Second Bedroom, 8 ft 6 ins × 11 ft 5 ins.   Third Bedroom, 7 ft 8 ins × 8 ft 6 ins   Linen Closet

Total cost, including all extras, £230 per cottage. Cubical contents, 33,918 ft at 3¼d. per ft cube   £460, or £230 each. (Built in 1899.)

The stairs in this instance descend to the entrance lobby, but they may be planned the other way about in order to avoid the necessity of traversing the parlour to get to the bedrooms, and to insure children crying upstairs being heard in the living room or the scullery   This, however, would necessitate the cutting of 3 ft off the large front bedroom, while the respective spaces for the larder and the lobby below would be reversed, the position of the former being undesirable.

Ordinary roofing tiles and common bricks have been used The living room is boarded, and the scullery quarried.

It might be pointed out that there is but little scope for variety of plan in these smaller cottages. The variations must be obtained in the treatment of elevations   As already stated, to build cheaply the main point is to get the walls as long and straight as possible

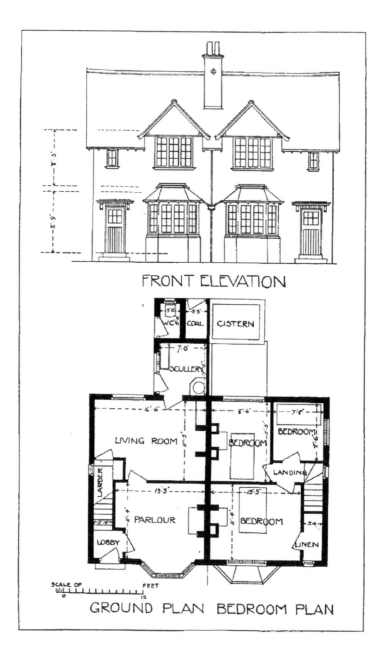

FRONT ELEVATION

GROUND PLAN BEDROOM PLAN

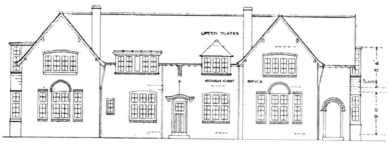

35

FRONT ELEVATION

SCALE OF   FEET

BLOCK OF THREE COTTAGES.

PLATES XXIX. AND XXX.

BLOCK OF THREE COTTAGES.

PLATE xxix. and the accompanying scale-drawing give the plan and elevation of a block of three cottages, a sketch of which appears in Plate xxx. The inner one occupies an exact third of the land, and is double fronted. By putting the inner one with its axis to the front, an equal garden space is given to all the houses without incurring a re-division of the land.

The inner and left-hand houses have practically the same accommodation, but the right-hand has several advantages : there is a wider hall, the living room is not a passage room, while the kitchen is reached from the hall, and the wash-house is entered from the yard.

Accommodation of *left-hand* and *inner* houses.

GROUND FLOOR.

    Parlour, 11 ft. 4 ins. × 15 ft. 3 ins. Living Room, 10 ft. × 14 ft. 6 ins. and bay. Scullery, 10 ft. × 6 ft. and recess for Bath. Coals, Tools, and w.c.

BEDROOM FLOOR.

    First Bedroom, 11 ft. 4 ins. × 15 ft. 3 ins. Second Bedroom, 7 ft. 6 ins. × 14 ft. 6 ins., and bay. Third Bedroom, 7 ft. 5 ins. × 11 ft. 6 ins. Fourth Bedroom, 9 ft. 6 ins. × 6 ft. (middle house only). Linen Closet.

Cost of left-hand and inner houses, including all extras, £293 per cottage   (Built in 1904)

The right-hand house, owing to the extra conveniences, works out at rather more

In the middle house the recess between the range and small window makes a very convenient space for a writing table, especially if curtains are dropped from a rod to screen it off, its proximity to the range making it a warm and cosy retreat in winter.   There is a bay window to the living room of the outside houses

Two of the houses in this block are fitted with Cornes' Patent Combined Scullery-Bath-Range and Boiler, described on page 52, and the third with the "Cabinet" bath.

The elevation, with the forecourt formed by the projection of the two outside houses, may be made very pleasing.   From the perspective it will be seen that the inner house is covered with roughcast, making an agreeable contrast with the outer ones of plain brickwork.   Roughcast, while fairly economical, is very effective, and helps to brighten the forecourt   The projection of the outer houses affords a break, the abruptness of which does not attract attention, but which gives an opportunity of stopping the roughcast, which would otherwise have to be carried round to the back of the whole block

It is not advisable to introduce a variety of colour upon exteriors   Colour is best disposed in masses— that is, it should be treated broadly, not distributed in isolated portions, or in sharply contrasting tints   (See page 59.)

The roof of this block is of green slates of varying sizes, diminishing towards the ridge

Aspect in the placing of the house is here studied as well as the site.   The axis runs south-west and north-east, and the front commands a pleasing perspective of one of the principal Bournville roads, and an admirable view of the Lickey Hills in the distance.

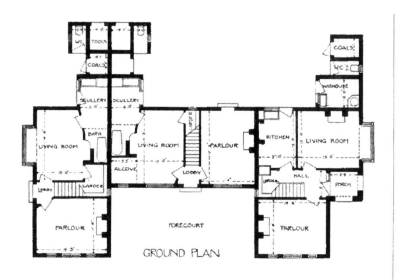

GROUND PLAN

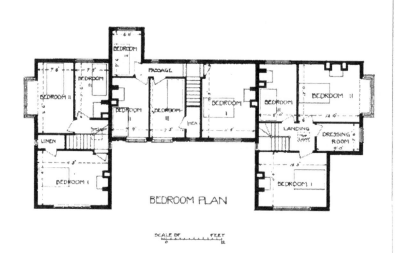

BEDROOM PLAN

SCALE OF   FEET

PLATE XXX . . . .
BLOCK OF THREE
COTTAGES. SEE
PAGE 35 . . . .

DESCRIPTIONS OF PLATES XXXI—XXXIII

PLATE XXXI
PAIR OF COTTAGES (SHALLOW SITE)

THE view shown in this plate illustrates the treatment of a shallow corner site, the block being a pair of semi-detached, double-fronted cottages.   The plan is similar to the middle house of the foregoing block.

PLATE XXXII
PAIR OF COTTAGES

A PAIR of cottages also planned on the same lines as the middle house shown in Plate XXIX. and the foregoing shallow-site pair, but placed at right-angles instead of lengthwise, and occupying a corner position

PLATE XXXIII
PAIR OF COTTAGES

AN example of a pair of cottages treated in the Dutch style.

PLATE XXXI. ·
PAIR OF COT-
TAGES. SEE · .
PAGE 38. . .

II

PLATE XXXII.
PAIR OF COT-

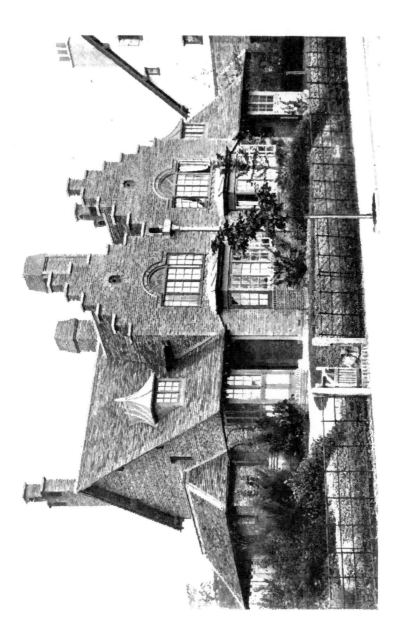

PLATE XXXIII.
PAIR OF COT-
TAGES. SEE
PAGE 38.

DESCRIPTION OF PLATES XXXIV. AND XXXV

40

PLATE XXXIV

PAIR OF COTTAGES

THE accommodation of the pair of cottages shown in this plate is
as follows :—

GROUND FLOOR.

Parlour, 11 ft 4 ins × 13 ft 6 ins, and bay   Living room, 11 ft 6 ins ×
14 ft 5 ins (French Windows)   Kitchen 10 ft 8 ins × 12 ft 3 ins.
Larder   Porch, Hall, and Clock Space under stairs   Tools, w c, and Coals
(Enclosed yard)

BEDROOM FLOOR.

First Bedroom, 11 ft 4 ins. × 13 ft 6 ins   Second Bedroom, 11 ft 6 ins ×
14 ft 5 ins   Third Bedroom, 8 ft 6 ins × 10 ft 8 ins.   Bath Room (hot and
cold water)

Height of rooms   Ground floor. 8 ft 9 ins , first floor,
8 ft. 6 ins

Total cost, including all extras, £375 per cottage

Laying out of gardens, £12 10s. each.

Cubical contents, 34, 285ft., at $5\frac{1}{4}d.$ per foot cube = £375 per
cottage   (Built in 1903)

MATERIALS.—Whitewashed common bricks are here used.
Whitewash is cheap and may be used very effectively, especially
where there are trees in the background   The roofs and dormers
are hipped, and covered with Welsh green slates and blue half-
round ridges , the chimney-pots are buff-colour.

SILLS.—The sills, as in many of the other houses, are formed
of calf-nosed bricks set on edge in cement, with two courses of
tiles beneath, which form a drip under the sill, and with a backing
of slate in cement   By bringing the window-frame forward to
reduce the size of the top of the sill, damp and the driving in
of rain are prevented   This makes an inexpensive sill, and adds
to the homely appearance of the cottage

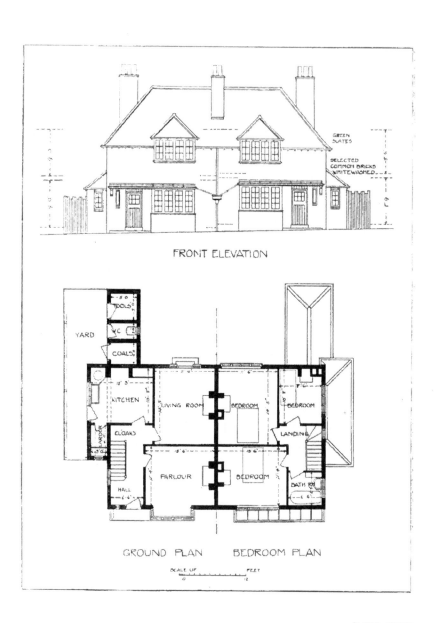

FRONT ELEVATION

GROUND PLAN   BEDROOM PLAN

SCALE OF   FEET

PLATE XXXIV.
PAIR OF COT-
TAGES SEE
PAGE 40.

INTERIOR WALL DECORATION —The interior wall decoration is duresco throughout Plain ingrain paper, of which there is a number of very cheap kinds now on the market, might be used with a frieze A good effect is obtained by bringing down the white from the ceiling as far as the picture rail, which gives light to the room and improves its proportions

The exterior woodwork is painted a Verona green

FIREPLACES —Fireplaces suitable for this or any of the six-roomed cottages are as follows .—

Front Room interior grate, slabbed surrounds, tiled hearth, and white wood chimney piece Living Room iron tiled mantel-sham Kitchen 3 ft range with white tiled coves and York stone shelf and trusses Front Bedroom 30 in mantel-sham and tiled hearth Back Bedrooms 24 in mantel-sham and tiled hearth

The total cost of the whole should not amount to more than £12

The scullery is lengthened by a projection in the nature of a bay The outbuildings, which are carried to right and left of the pair, give privacy to the garden near to the houses

PLATE XXXV
PAIR OF COTTAGES

THIS plate illustrates one of several different treatments of the last plan

PLATES XXXVI, XXXVII, AND XXXVIII

SINGLE COTTAGE

PLATE XXXVI gives the plan of a single cottage occupying a corner site It contains:—

GROUND FLOOR

Drawing Room, 12 ft 6 ins × 13 ft 6 ins, and bay   Dining Room, 13 ft × 13 ft, and bay (French casements)   Kitchen, 10 ft × 11 ft   Scullery, 8 ft × 10 ft   Larder   Porch and Hall, with Cloak Space under stairs   Coals, Tools, and w c

BEDROOM FLOOR.

First Bedroom, 13 ft 6 ins × 15 ft 9 ins   Second Bedroom, 11 ft 6 ins × 13 ft   Third Bedroom, 10 ft × 13 ft   Dressing Room   Cupboards. Bathroom, with w c and Lavatory (hot and cold water)

As will be seen, there is very little space wasted in the planning of the rooms

The whole of the exterior is rough-cast. The front bedroom is enlarged and projects over the ground floor, giving a pleasant shade to the lower portion of the elevation, while the roof is continued over one side and carried down to form the porch. The gable is of half-timber framing.

The roof is covered with Hartshill hand-made tiles, which, while richly toning and colouring, have admirably stood the test of several years' hard weather, and have proved much more durable than the pressed tile used for some of the other cottages at Bournville.

The plan of the cottage might be simplified by gabling back and front, the roof thus covering the whole building, and having no valleys. The bedroom accommodation could be then increased by the addition of attics.

Two views of the actual example appear in PLATES XXXVII and XXXVIII

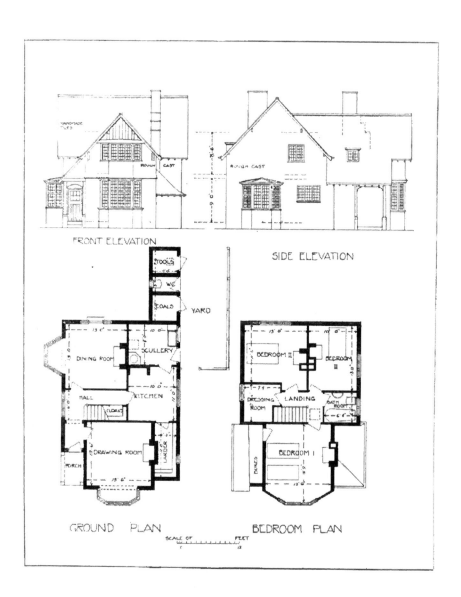

FRONT ELEVATION

SIDE ELEVATION

GROUND PLAN

BEDROOM PLAN

SCALE OF FEET

PLATE XXXVI.
SINGLE COT-
TAGE. SEE.
PAGE 42.

PLATE XXXVII.
SINGLE COTTAGE.

PLATE XXXVIII.

DESCRIPTIONS OF PLATES XXXIX.—XLII.

PLATES XXXIX, XL, XLI, AND XLII

SINGLE COTTAGE

ANOTHER single cottage has accommodation as follows :—

GROUND FLOOR

> Living Room, including roomy alcove, 13 ft 5 ins × 15 ft. 6 ins Kitchen, 10 ft × 13 ft. 5 ins Scullery, Larder, Tools, w c, Coals, and Enclosed Yard

BEDROOM FLOOR.

> First Bedroom, 13 ft 5 ins × 15 ft 6 ins Second Bedroom, 10 ft × 13 ft 5 ins Third Bedroom, 9 ft 6 ins × 9 ft 6 ins. Bathroom (hot and cold water) and w c
>
> Spacious Attic (shown by dotted lines) and Boxrooms

Total cost, in 1903. £540.

Cubical contents, 19,938 ft., at $6\frac{1}{2}d.$ per ft. cube, £540.

By hanging a curtain, the alcove shown in the plan may be made private for writing or studying, if required. It may also be used for meals ; and if a door communicates with the hall, the table may be laid by the maid unseen by the visitor, and the curtains afterwards drawn apart Thus one of the disadvantages urged against the larger-sized houses with one large living room may be overcome.

MATERIALS.—The cottage is built of whitewashed common bricks, with tarred plinth, the roof being covered with Peake's dark brindled hand-made roofing tiles It is without decoration, apart from what is afforded by the semicircular hood over the front door, the wrought-iron brackets supporting the gutters, and at the back a semicircular arch to give importance to the living room. There are shutters to all the ground-floor windows, which are made to bolt from within.

The view shown in PLATE XL. is of the back.

PLATES XLI and XLII show the staircase and dining room respectively.

FRONT ELEVATION   BACK ELEVATION

HANDMADE
BRINDLED
TILES

COMMON
BRICKS
WHITE
WASHED

TOOLS

WC

KITCHEN   LIVING ROOM

COALS

YARD

SCULLERY   HALL   ALCOVE

LARDER   PORCH

GROUND PLAN

BEDROOM   BEDROOM

WC   LANDING

BATH ROOM   BEDROOM

DOTTED
LINES
SHOW
ATTIC

BEDROOM PLAN

SCALE OF   FEET

PLATE XXXIX. . .
SINGLE COTTAGE.
SEE PAGE 44. . .

PLATE XL. . . . .
SINGLE COTTAGE. .
BACK. SEE PAGE 44.

PLATE XLI. . . .
STAIRCASE OF . .
SINGLE COTTAGE.
SEE PAGE 44. . .

DESCRIPTIONS OF PLATES XLIII AND XLIV.

PLATES XLIII AND XLIV.

SINGLE COTTAGE

PLATES XLIII and XLIV show the plan and view respectively of another type of single cottage, with the following accommodation —

GROUND FLOOR.

> Dining Room, 13 ft × 19 ft, and small alcove   Drawing Room, 13 ft × 16 ft 6 ins, and bay   Kitchen, 9 ft 6 ins × 15 ft
>
> Scullery, 8 ft 6 ins × 9 ft 4 ins   Larder, Coals, Ashes, w c, and Enclosed Yard

BEDROOM FLOOR.

> First Bedroom, 13 ft × 13 ft 4 ins   Second Bedroom, 12 ft × 13 ft, and large bay   Third Bedroom, 9 ft 6 ins × 12 ft   Fourth Bedroom, 8 ft 6 ins × 13 ft 4 ins   Bathroom, with Lavatory and w c   Large Attic, extending over almost the whole of the four rooms

Total cost, in 1904, £640   Cubical contents, 25,077 ft. at 6⅛d. per ft cube = £640.

By the arrangement of the stairs it will be noticed that additional space is secured to the dining room, forming a pleasant arched alcove

MATERIALS —The materials used are brindled bricks, Peake's hand-made roofing tiles, hips and ridges covered with half-round ridge-tiles, 6 in. half-round spouts with ornamental stays, projecting hood of timber, covered with lead and supported by two wrought-iron stays, red tall-boy chimney pots, doors painted Suffield green, window sashes and frames ivory white, and eaves, gutters and down-spouts lead colour

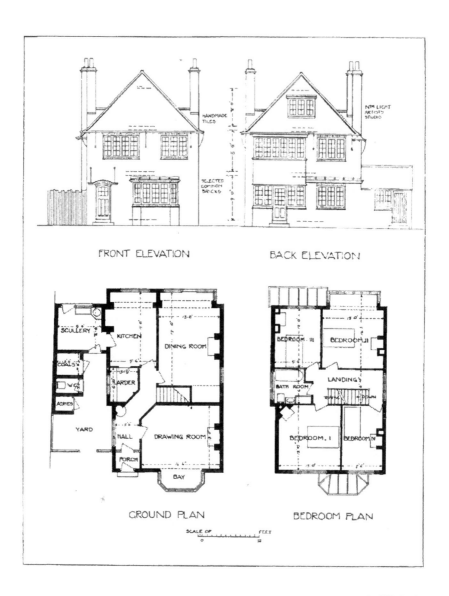

FRONT ELEVATION   BACK ELEVATION

GROUND PLAN   BEDROOM PLAN

SCALE OF   FEET

PLATE XLIII.
SINGLE COT-
TAGE. SEE
PAGE 46

K

PLATE XLIV.
SINGLE COT-
TAGE. SEE
PAGE 46

PLATES XLV, XLVI, AND XLVII

PAIR OF THREE STOREY COTTAGES

PLATES XIV. and XLVI. give plans, and PLATE XLVII the view of a pair of three-storey cottages of about the same accommodation, the left-hand having the following :—

GROUND FLOOR.

> Dining Room, 11 ft 6 ins × 18 ft, with French window Drawing Room, 12 ft 6 ins × 15 ft, with deep bay Small Sitting Room, 7 ft × 11 ft 2 ins Working Kitchen, 11 ft 2 in × 12 ft 6 ins Larder and China Pantry, Porch and Hall w c, Coals, Tools, and Enclosed Yard

BEDROOM FLOOR

> First Bedroom, 12 ft 6 ins × 15 ft, and deep bay Second Bedroom 11 ft 6 ins × 16 ft Third Bedroom, 10 ft 6 ins × 11 ft 2 ins, with oriel Bathroom, with Lavatory, w c Two Attics and Large Box Room

The accommodation in the two houses differs owing to the aspect. If the two plans were identical, a considerable portion of the right-hand garden would be shut off from the south, and the larder would not face the north Stress has already been laid on the necessity of considering aspect

The left-hand is a corner house, and the projecting out-houses answer the double purpose of screening the garden from the road and protecting the house from the north wind

In the adjoining house there is no small sitting-room, but an extra attic The out-buildings are attached to the main building, and do not project into the garden; the principal room is thus left open to the south.

MATERIALS.—The houses are built of common bricks white-washed, with a tarred plinth. There are half-timber porches, and the spaces between the bays and under the dormers are covered with rough-cast and decorated with parquetry. The rainwater head in front is picked out in vermillion, the introduction of a very little bright colour giving a pleasant jewel-like effect Peake's hand-made tiles, of dark colour, are used for the roofs, with half-round ridging, and ornamental iron stays support the gutters, which are of 6 in half-round iron

A pair of houses erected to a similar plan to that of the right-hand house in 1904 cost £610 each The cost of the examples given work out more owing to the fall in the land, which necessitates very deep footings, and also to the plans differing in order to suit aspect and site.

PLATE XLVIII
PAIR OF THREE STOREY COTTAGES

PLATE xlviii gives the view of a pair of houses similar to the last, but somewhat reduced in size, and the treatment varied. Brindled bricks are used for the ground floor, and rough-cast for the upper storeys.

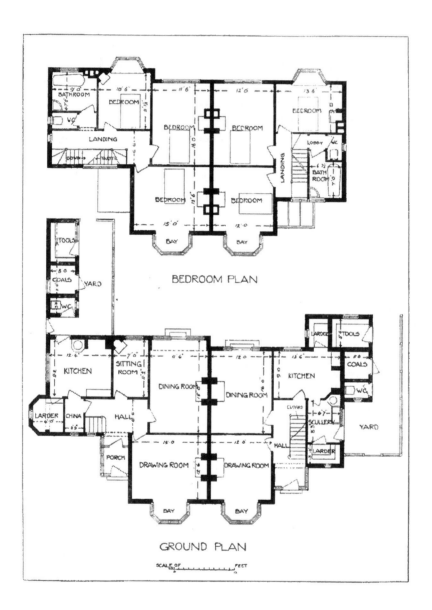

BEDROOM PLAN

GROUND PLAN

SCALE OF FEET

PLATE XLV. . .
PAIR OF COT-
TAGES. SEE .
PAGE 47 . . .

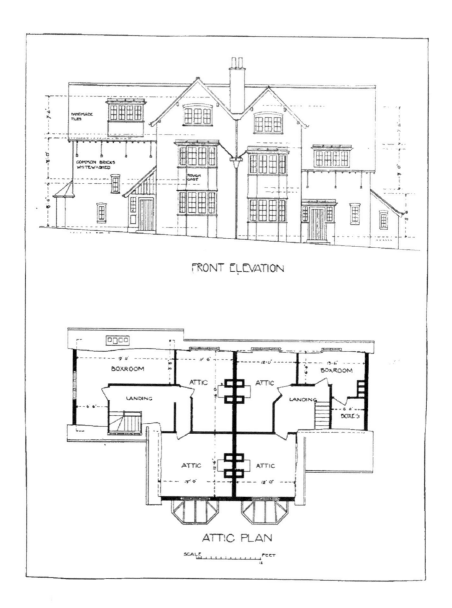

FRONT ELEVATION

ATTIC PLAN

SCALE FEET

PLATE XLVI. . .
PAIR OF COT-
TAGES. SEE . .
PAGE 47 . . . .

PLATE XLVII.
PAIR OF COT-
TAGES. SEE
PAGE 47.

PLATES XLIX , L , LI , LII , LIII , LIV , AND LV

TWO PAIRS OF COTTAGES

THESE plates illustrate two pairs of cottages of two storeys each, almost identical in plan, but differently treated

The accommodation of the pair shown in PLATES XLIX and L. is :—

GROUND FLOOR.

Dining Room, 13 ft 6 in × 16 ft and bay 16 ft 3 ins , including ingle and bay window Hall, with storm doors, 12 ft 6 ins × 10 ft and Tool House Frontage, 15 yds

Drawing Room, 13 ft 6 ins × Kitchen, 10 ft 6 ins × 12 ft Scullery, Larder, w c , Coals,

BEDROOM FLOOR.

First Bedroom, 12 ft × 16 ft 3 ins , and bay × 13 ft 6 in Third Bedroom, 10 ft × 10 ft 2 ins 9 ft × 13 ft 6 ins Boxroom, 8 ft × 10 ft Bathroom, with Lavatory, and w c

Second Bedroom, 12 ft 4 ins Fourth Bedroom,

The dining room is lighted by a small east window and a west bay window, the latter being covered by the roof of the verandah. which terminates in the bay window of the drawing room. Although the kitchen is a small one, it has the advantage of not being a passage room, the door from the hall to the kitchen and that from the kitchen to the scullery being arranged beside one another in the same wall. In these houses the windows have wooden frames and wrought-iron casements.

The principal rooms occupy the full width of the back, and the hall is therefore extended to admit of the doors of the two rooms being conveniently placed.

INGLE-NOOK —The ingle which results from this arrangement has a beam with a shelf above continuing the line of the architrave, and the ceiling of the ingle is only 6ft. 6 in high   There is a small light on one side

The ingle-nook is shown on PLATE LI., and a view of the oriel on PLATE LII.

The pair of cottages shown in PLATES LIII. and LIV have outer porches, whereby the size of the hall is reduced A separate view of one of them is given on PLATE IV

In this example, as in the former also, the outlook at the back of the house is to be preferred to that in the front, and as should always be done when the aspect is favourable, the principal rooms are placed at the back There is in this instance a west prospect, with a delightful view of undulating woodland and distant hills The forecourt affords a pleasant outlook from within the house. The lowness of the eaves has the effect of giving the pair a very homely and cottage-like appearance The height of the bedrooms in the former example is 8 ft 3 in.

PLATES LVI AND LVII
SINGLE COTTAGE

PLATE LVI. gives a single cottage of a plan similar to the last, with enlarged accommodation and somewhat different treatment, namely .—

Rough-cast from ground, with tarred plinth ; oriel window to first floor, with the introduction of a little colour in parquetry, which is also applied round the small window over the entrance, and a half-timber porch glazed with leaded lights, having coloured centres of rich glass. The cloak space is here converted into a china pantry

A separate view of the porch is shown on PLATE LVII

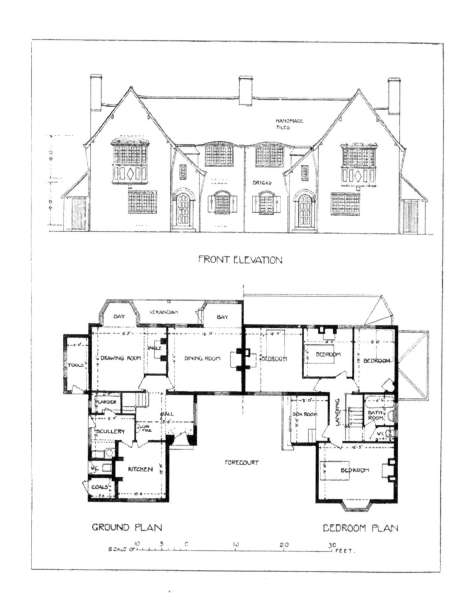

FRONT ELEVATION

GROUND PLAN

BEDROOM PLAN

SCALE OF [10 5 0 10 20 30] FEET.

PLATE LI . . . .

PLATE LII. . .
DETAIL VIEW.
SEE PAGE 49

PLATE LIV. :
PAIR OF COT-
TAGES—BACK. :
SEE PAGE 50. :

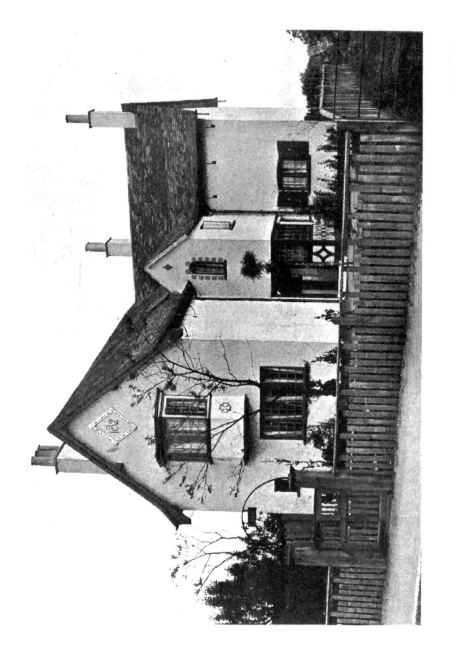

PLATE LVI.

SINGLE COT-

PLATE LVII. .
PORCH OF . .
SINGLE COT. .
TAGE. SEE .
PAGE 50 . . .

M

GENERAL NOTES.

THE BATH.—The bath, without which no house is nowadays regarded as complete, should be supplied in all cottages, however small. At Bournville, wherever there is no bathroom, the bath is placed in the kitchen, this room being considered the most suitable: hot water is here at hand, and, as there is usually a fire in winter, it is both more convenient and comfortable than in one of the bedrooms, where the space can be ill-spared, especially where there are children. Even in the kitchens of these small cottages there is necessarily none too much space, and various devices have been employed to prevent the bath being an inconvenience when not in use. One way of disposing of it is to sink it into the floor near the hearth, the

THE PATENT ADJUSTABLE CABINET BATH.

boarded covering serving as a standing or draining board when the bath is in use. Another way, where there is a little more room to spare, is to fix it on the usual floor level, and make its cover serve as a settle or table. The intro-

M 2

duction of the Patent Adjustable Cabinet Bath, however, is better
than either of these methods. In this arrangement the bath is
hinged at the bottom of one end in order that it may be easily
lowered from and raised back into the cabinet, where in its vertical

CORNES' PATENT BATH.

position it is no
inconvenience when
not in use. In the
hinge a waste pipe is
introduced. With
this bath not only is
there a gain of space,
but the bath may be
used with a saving
of time and labour,
and without fear of
deluging the floor.
Above the cupboard
in which the bath is
kept are convenient
shelves. The cost of
the bath and cabinet
is about £3 5s.
The illustration on
the last page shows
a bath of this kind
fitted in one of the
Bournville cottages.

Another patent bath used at Bournville in cottages of larger
size but not sufficiently large to admit of a bathroom is Cornes'
Combined Scullery-Bath-Range and Boiler. The patent utilises to
the fullest extent the heat of the kitchen, so that, in addition to the

economy of space, there is a further economy of fuel to the house-holder   The heating and cooking range forms a great part of the division between the kitchen and scullery-bathroom, the flue being coursed over the head of the bath   In the centre of the range is the grate, with an oven on one side and on the other a twelve-gallon boiler, in which water is kept hot for domestic purposes. Boiling water can be obtained by raking down live fuel into a small secondary grate under the boiler through a small hole made for the purpose   If desired, clothes can be boiled in the boiler and access to it from the scullery may be gained by opening a curved door.   Owing to its open construction there is no risk of explosion.   Further developments have been made in the way of providing a folding door in front of the range, which will shut off the boiler from the kitchen when necessary   The scullery-bathroom, which contains about 36 superficial feet, is fitted with a full-sized iron enamelled bath, supplied with hot water through a pipe from the range boiler and with cold water from the cistern, or through a shower-bath sprinkler fixed overhead, so that this latter luxury can be enjoyed by simply turning the tap.   The introduction of White's Patent Steam Exhaust effectually prevents the steam from permeating the other rooms of the house.   An illustration is here given showing Cornes' patent fitted up.

THE INGLE-NOOK —Like many old-time features which have been revived during the last few years, the ingle-nook has perhaps been a little overdone.   The ingle is intended to serve as a cosy retreat in a spacious room, and it should not be introduced in a room the size of which is insufficient to warrant its existence   On this account it is usually undesirable to provide ingle-nooks in cottages, except in those with the large living-rooms. Comfort should always be the object in view in the construction of the ingle, but in many modern examples this is sacrificed to over

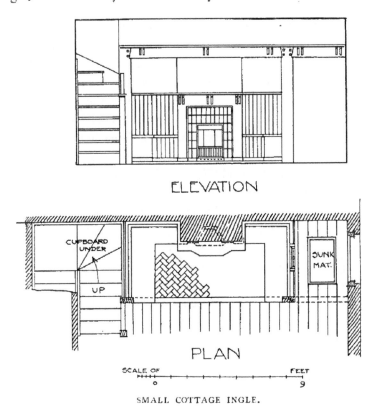

ELEVATION

PLAN

SCALE OF ⊢⊢⊦⊦ 0 FEET 9

SMALL COTTAGE INGLE.

elaboration and that straining for effect which shows that it was designed for ornament and not for use. No doubt an effect is sometimes gained, but the usefulness of the ingle is so far sacrificed that not infrequently one of most inviting appearance will be found to possess inadequate seating accommodation even for a single person.

The ingle, to be comfortable and useful, should not be less than 10 ft 6 ins in width by 4 ft 6 ins in depth If it is smaller lengthways the heat from the fire will be too great, while if less deep there will be insufficient accommodation at the sides for two persons without projecting the seats into the room, which can only be satisfactorily done, perhaps, when the side of the ingle is in line with that of the room. A reasonable height is 6 ft. 6 ins A pleasing way of treating a cottage ingle is to introduce a step up of about 3 ins, with an oak curb, and to tile or quarry the whole recess, as illustrated by the accompanying drawing This ingle, which is provided in the pair of cottages with the large living-rooms dealt with earlier (Plate xx), is constructed as follows :—$\frac{3}{4}$ in matchboarding is nailed to studding, which has stout angle-posts to support the beam above; along the side of the latter a 7-in by 1-in shelf is carried by small wooden brackets, and the wood seats are of $1\frac{1}{4}$ ins in thickness by 1 ft. 4 ins from back to front, at a height of 1 ft 3 ins. or less from the floor The introduction of the ingle here is advantageous because some privacy is thus afforded in a room which is entered directly from the road The match-boarding in this case is continued, and forms a framework for the tile-surround of the grate, giving an appearance of unity to the nook, while the simplicity of the material is pleasing and restful The insertion of a mantelpiece different in character should be avoided Some interest may be given to the centre of the fireplace by inlaying a little ebony in simple forms

.For drawing-rooms of larger houses the back of the nook might be panelled, the seat upholstered, and the panels filled in with tapestry. White wood looks well, and the fireplace might be built up with glazed brickettes The ways of treating the more expensive ingles are so numerous, however, that it would be of little use making definite suggestions

The ingle-nook of one of the larger cottages is illustrated on Plate 11.

CHIMNEYS.—The economy of grouping chimneys, and the desirability of carrying them to the highest point of the roof to avoid down-draughts, has already been mentioned Generally speaking, for cottages, the simpler the chimneys are the better, and they should all be of hard burnt bricks, and the top courses built in cement Diagonal chimneys are pleasing, but expensive, and on an estate should only be used occasionally The Dutch chimneys, built up with corners of brick and covered with stone slabs or 12-in. drain pipes, as frequently seen in Holland and Belgium, are picturesque (see Plate XXII.), but care has to be exercised in their construction Though they are often regarded as being liable to smoke, it may be pointed out that in many cases their employment is the only remedy for a smoky flue. Outside chimneys, it will be borne in mind, are always expensive Chimney pots do not improve the appearance, but sometimes they are a necessity In these cases the simple or plain tall-boys are recommended, and the colour—whether of soft red or buff—should be chosen to suit the design and colouring of the cottage As a variation of these there are the beehive pots, the main idea of which is to keep down the height.

WINDOWS.—The casement window is cheaper than the sash window, and if beauty of effect is also to be considered its adoption is further desirable Its simplicity and homeliness of appearance render it extremely fitting for the cottage The old difficulty of

cleaning may now be obviated by a very simple device introduced at Bournville, that of causing the window to open upon
a pivot in the centre, inwardly as well as outwardly, which
admits of the outside of the fixed pane being easily reached by the
hand.

The sash window, while objectionable in the form frequently
used, may yet be made suitable for cottages, but it should be
divided, and the proportions very carefully studied, say 9 in by
11-in. panes, and the bars not less than 1 in in thickness It
should be brought forward, showing the full width of the boxing
The sash window, however, necessitates an additional height
to rooms

BRICKS —As regards bricks, it is well as far as possible to avoid
those which are mechanically made (the pressed stock-brick) and to
use the hand-made bricks from local yards. The brindled Stafford-
shire bricks are largely used at Bournville , they are very suitable
for cottage building where the position is not too exposed A
pleasing variety of colour is introduced at a low cost, the tint being
a bright cherry red blended with blue and purple, the blue being
quite different from the dead blue-black of the vitreous brick
For inside work the common red wire-cuts are suitable

It is a mistake to suppose that a good effect cannot be obtained
by the use of the cheaper makes of bricks, a remark which also
applies in the case of the London stock-bricks, so long as they are
not uniformly selected , a good effect may be gained, for instance,
by using a few of the darker ones indiscriminately with the cream-
coloured ones. The splash of dark colour caused by the black ones
coming together is by no means undesirable A good example of

an effective use of these bricks is to be seen at Brewer's Estate,
London

Roof Covering —The materials to be employed in roofing
depend upon the style of cottage, and also upon the locality   The
Bangor slates are cheap, and may be an excellent covering as
regards durability , but unfortunately , in the class of cottages here
dealt with, it is rarely possible to get so good an effect with them as
with other kinds   They may be used, however, in the whitewashed
cottage, so long as the smaller sizes are selected   Hand-made roofing
tiles, and thick Welsh green and rustic Precelly slates may be
recommended, as also the Peake's & Hartshill hand-made tiles

Pantiles are cheap, but should only be employed on unbroken
roofs having few valleys, where it is less difficult to keep out the
wet   The roof should be steep, the angle in no case being less
than 45 degrees   Before covering, care should be taken to
ascertain whether they are of good manufacture, and whether they
are porous or not.   There are sometimes pantiles of an indifferent
quality on the market , and, if this precaution is not taken, a roof
may have to be stripped and re-tiled.   Where they have been used
and have afterwards been found to be bad they may be tarred, as
are wood coverings in Norway and Sweden.   It is always essential
that the services of a practised layer of pantiles should be secured

Gables should have damp courses under the coping to shield
them from frost and wet

Roof ridging should have careful attention, and it is wiser to
suppress rather than to sharpen, the better to obtain that rustic
appearance suitable to a cottage   Many fantastic ridges, with
vulgar finials, are employed in the building of small suburban villas,
of a more or less sharp-pointed character, and of a depth out of

proportion to the roof, which gives an unpleasant harshness to the
general appearance. With the principle in view that the sky-line
should be softened as much as possible, the brindled hand-made
half-rounds should be used. With green slates, ridges of blue are
the most suitable, as the colours harmonise. Experience will
probably show that the red and buff ridges will not stand the
weather so well as other kinds.

WALL SPACES : ROUGH-CAST—WHITEWASH—HALF-TIMBER —
However strong may be the temptation to introduce a variety
of colour upon exteriors, it is advisable with cottages of the class
dealt with to refrain from so doing. It is best to get the colour in
masses, treated broadly—say, each house, as far as wall surfaces and
roof are concerned, of one colour, for where the cottages stand
close together, or even where they are semi-detached, sufficient
contrast or relief is afforded by contiguous cottages treated
differently, and in the case of a village a much better general effect
is thus gained. On the other hand a good effect may be gained
by giving a block of houses one tone throughout, matching the
colour of the roof. The result is quiet and unobtrusive, and one
which is very desirable in the cottage, where the features are
necessarily brought close together. The tarred plinth, however,
should always be used with rough-cast

Half-timber should be used sparingly. While the bye-laws
insist on a 9-in wall being at the back, an unwarranted present
and future expense is incurred by its use ; and an effect equally
as good, moreover, may be obtained with rough-cast, weather
boarding, or whitewash. Half-timber one lives to regret, for the
weather tells sadly upon it, and it demands constant repair

A small cottage with an equal distribution of equal-sized windows is far from desirable. In a pair of cottages where there are four equal rooms facing the road, four equal windows would at first sight seem unavoidable, although such an arrangement would be fatal to the elevation   It is better to put a secondary light to the rooms at the extremities, getting additional light from the side, and thus by contrast giving greater importance to the larger windows in the centre, or even to omit the smaller windows, if adequate light can be obtained without them The blank space might then be used for the training up of climbing plants   A certain number of windows is indispensable in a cottage, but, without stinting light, the aim should rather be to repress any superfluity. By the means suggested the view from the interior is sometimes agreeably varied.

Other features are dealt with in the descriptions of the various cottages to which they have particular reference

THE LAYING OUT OF A MODEL VILLAGE

LET it be supposed that land has been bought to be laid out as a model village Whether this has been done by a company, a municipal body, or by an individual, is not material to the present purpose. Assuming that the selection of the site has had careful consideration, and that it is suitable for the development of a village, what is the first step? Before turning a sod the clearest conception of the finished scheme must have been formed. A dozen cottages or so erected before considering the future of the whole project may involve endless trouble at a later stage. The initial proceeding, therefore, is to make the general plan as complete and final as possible before commencing actual operations Up to the present it has been the difficulty of co operation among landlords, perhaps unavoidable, either by the piecemeal acquisition of land or the fitful demand for building, which has been the cause of many of our towns and suburbs being the reverse of pleasing A century or so ago, when domestic architecture was a traditionally living art, and building was conducted less hurriedly, a certain charm of effect was no doubt obtained by this accidental or fitful extension, though convenience was certainly not always considered ; but in the present day we should avail ourselves of the opportunity which a large or co-operative scheme offers for a convenient and agreeable disposition of buildings.

REGARD OF PHYSICAL FEATURES —As the following suggestions do not refer to any specific example of land which is to be laid out as a model village, they can only be regarded as having

general applicability. The treatment of particular land depends
upon its peculiar physical features   Land in a gently undulating
district, for instance, must be dealt with in quite a different
manner from that in flat country   The natural features themselves must be the basis of any satisfactory treatment, and they
are to be made the most of, not only with regard to their intrinsic
beauty, but also any material advantages they may offer.

ADVISORY ARCHITECT —If a village is being developed by an
individual in a private capacity it is not improbable, indeed it is
very natural, that he will expect the general operations to be
carried out in accordance with his particular taste or fancy, which,
however, may happen to be far from practical or artistic, and his
scheme is likely to suffer accordingly.   So too in the case of an
estate developed by a governing body consisting of men who are
not qualified for the task, the possibility of failure is equally great.
The best course is to employ an advisory architect about whose
qualifications there is no doubt, who should work in conjunction
with the surveyor from the outset.   It may be suggested, now that
the movement is making considerable progress, that the Royal
Institute of British Architects should be asked to suggest an
architect in such cases   A greater variety, however, in the plan
and design of the houses might perhaps be secured by employing
more than one architect.   A man's ideas are liable to run in a
groove , and even if variation is introduced in detail there is likely
to be a similarity in general character   Moreover, where two or
more architects are engaged, a healthy rivalry might result in the
designing of houses which shall fulfil all the conditions of convenience, compactness, and economy.   The respective work of the
various architects might be confined to particular streets, but a
regular system of variation should be avoided   Method should
not be too obtrusive or the arrangement too mechanical   The

advisory architect must be selected with judgment, for on him will devolve the working out of the general road-scheme, and this will demand more talent than the merely practical man possesses

The caution already urged against doing anything on the estate without mature consideration expressly applies to the cutting of roads and the reservation of spaces. Given a map of our land, the fancy is not usually slow in disposing of it , and it is only with the progress of operations, when a number of unforeseen demands make themselves disagreeably formidable, that it is seen how wanton this ready fancy has been.

THE SELECTION OF CENTRES.—The first questions to be decided are the number and positions of the centres, for it is to and from these that the most convenient and accessible connections must be planned, and the centres themselves should be reserved as the sites of parks, principal buildings, shops and the like

If the land is already entered by one or more turnpike roads which may not be diverted, these should guide the cutting of the new roads, and the chief centres of the village must be made as accessible as possible from them. If an existing road only approaches the land, and only one connection is deemed necessary, the connection should be constructed to suit the village as a whole, without partiality to any one extremity, always keeping the centres in view. It is nearly always better to work to the contour of the land, taking a gentle sweep in preference to a straight line.

The site of the chief centre, not forgetting to keep in view its general accessibility, should if possible be on the highest point of the village, such a position giving prominence over the whole, as well as a more imposing elevation and dignity to the principal buildings which are to be erected thereon. The nature of the buildings would depend altogether on the size of the scheme. In the case of a garden city they would possibly include council

chambers, theatre, museum, library or other monumental buildings
of a like character, and as large spaces as possible should be reserved
around them for extensions and gardens.   A great city, in which it
has been decided to build a cathedral, has found itself before now
in the dilemma of having no suitable site available, and the monument of beauty has had to make the best of beggarly and ugly
neighbours   It is as well to profit by the errors of the past, and
the utmost should therefore be done to save a garden city or model
village from ever getting congested at its chief centre.

The other centres should be places of distinct interest, such as
schools, railway station, or market-place, but secondary to the chief
one

ROADS —The buildings will not be sky-scrapers, and the roads,
therefore, will not, in order that they may be ventilated, have to be
set out in straight lines in order to be wind-swept, intersecting at
unpleasing right angles like a gridiron   Though the main streets
should be planned with some degree of straightness for the convenience of getting to and from important places, there is no reason
why regularity should be sought after for its own sake ; at the same
time an unnecessary irregularity should be as much avoided.
Where one straight road unavoidably meets another at right angles,
it is a good plan to widen the point of intersection   This particu-
larly applies to a road taking a hill straight—that is, at its shortest
length   A pleasing perspective will be given by thus widening,
and on the triangular space formed might be erected a fountain or
monument, with or without a grass plot.   As an alternative, if the
ground is too valuable to be so disposed of, the road might be ter-
minated by slightly curving it to the left or right, and the corner
remaining used for building upon.   In the residential portion of
the village or garden city, roads running due east and west should
be avoided if possible   When this precaution has been taken,

much scheming to get the sun on the front as well as the back of the house will be spared As is well known, a kitchen with a south aspect is unbearable in the heat of the summer. Where the road unavoidably runs east and west, the gardens of houses on the north side should occupy the front and not the back of the plot

Trees should be planted in all roads, and the chief roads should be arranged on the boulevard plan, allowing the utmost freedom to the pedestrian A few spaces might be reserved for shelters, and the site for a bandstand might be timely chosen. As much as possible should be done to give breadth to all thoroughfares, and to this end the building-line of the houses should be well back from the road—thirty feet at least—the ample front-garden giving a refreshing greenness to the prospect, besides a better perspective to the houses. The width of roads should be from forty to fifty feet, with paths of from eight to twelve feet, not less

Minor open spaces, such as playgrounds for young children, are pleasant along the road side, but road-making is costly, and economy in all probability will have to be studied , back land, therefore, should be utilised for them at the bottom of garden plots

STREET ELEVATIONS —In building a road of houses the expense would of course be considerable if to get variety a different plan and different details were employed for each house Other methods must be adopted In the case of twenty houses it would be well to get as many details, such as windows, doors, and door-frames, the same (or, at any rate, half of one kind and half of another), and monotony should be avoided by variation in the disposition of these features An extensive elevation may also be made interesting by the treatment of a porch here, the addition of a bay window there, and the use of rough-cast somewhere else An irregular building-line, where possible, is

N

to be preferred. In a block of three cottages a pleasing effect is gained by projecting or recessing the middle one, or putting it with its long axis parallel with the road, and so forming a forecourt in front

SERVICE OF NATURAL ADVANTAGES — Whatever natural advantages the land may possess, such as woods, pools, or streams (where they are not included in a park), should border, or be seen from, the road—that is if they merit the expense of road-making. Few things are more picturesque than a stream at the roadside (as at Tissington in Derbyshire), especially if spanned here and there by small bridges (as at Bourton-on-the-Water), and by their presence the road will be widened from house front to house front   The water of a stream should never be utilised for a manufacturing purpose where it afterwards flows through the village, except for generating electric power or other clean uses   If there is an avenue of old trees it should be secured for one of the roads

SHOPPING.—The chief shopping will be best placed just without and surrounding the main centre, and that of less importance round the minor centres.

FACTORIES —Supposing that the *raison d'etre* of the village or garden city be one or more industries in which many of the inhabitants are employed, where, it will be asked, are the factories to be placed ? Without a definite example of land, it is difficult to give a definite reply.   Many things are essential to such sites—for instance, the adjacency of a stream, river, or railway—and if the manufacturer transfers his works to the country, he will rightly choose the most convenient and advantageous site for them that offers, and other arrangements will have to be made in concert with him   Nevertheless, the factory or factories should be as far as possible from the main centre, that is on the village or city outskirts The preferable position would lie between the north-east and south-west, for the prevalent south west wind will then carry away the smoke in summer, when the villagers indulge in outdoor life, while the north and easterly winds of winter will carry it over the village when they are indoors Screens of trees should be planted between the village and the factories as soon as possible.

PLOTS FOR HOUSES.—As to the treatment of the plots for houses · should the road cut into the land it need not necessarily be levelled, but taken as it is , the gables will thus present a desirable variation of level, and the ridge line will be less monotonous An endeavour should be made, however, always to get the plots not less than 18 ins. above the level of the crown of the road, otherwise the drainage will be troublesome and expensive.

As soon as the house is erected, it is well to set hedges of thorn or beech, both along the roadside and between the houses Until these are grown, the ordinary iron hurdle, or light-railed wooden fence, might serve.

It is advisable to arrange the building plots so that the houses on either side of the road do not come exactly opposite each other, the houses should be so arranged as to face the open space opposite

GARDENS —At Bournville the average garden-space allowed each house is 600 square yards, this being found to be about as much as the average man can well attend to (This means there will be from eight to twelve cottages to the acre) The laying out is done prior to the tenant's occupation of the house. A description of the way the Bournville gardens are laid out is given, with a plan, on page 23.

When the houses are placed at the end of the plot remote from the road any hard and fast lines in the style of the garden should be avoided · apple and other fruit-trees, or an occa-

sional kitchen-garden, may be placed in a prominent position, for
even the trim flower garden might be varied with advantage. A
preference has already been expressed for having the garden adjacent
to the house rather than the allotment garden at a distance, but at
the same time the latter plan may be sometimes forced upon us.
Undoubtedly the rivalry that is encouraged among gardeners con-
gregated together in allotment gardens is good and healthy, but
the inconvenience to the household of the distance between home
and garden would suggest the adoption of the former whenever it
is possible, and even where there is an allotment there should still
be a small plot adjacent to the house

While endeavouring to get as much light and air space as
possible in the village, it will frequently be found necessary to
erect cottages in blocks of four, and sometimes of eight.   In order
to give adequate garden-space, even to small houses, and not in
long thin strips, the frontage of the land will have to be broad,
a rule should be made, therefore, of spreading the houses laterally
by arranging the staircase of each house, not between the back and
front rooms, but between the houses   This will bring the outside
houses nearer to the extremity of the land, and will not only give
each garden the desired straightness and breadth, but afford a
greater breadth of view upon it from within.

In conclusion, it might be again stated that most of the
remarks under this head—which are mainly arranged from notes
taken or suggested during the planning and working out of the
Bournville Estate—are broad and suggestive rather than insistent,
and it is probable that the setting out of particular land will not
admit of the adoption of many of the principles here laid down

BRADBURY, AGNEW & CO LD , PRINTERS, LONDON AND TONBRIDGE